THE STORY BEHIND THE SYMBOL

NATIONAL ANTHEM

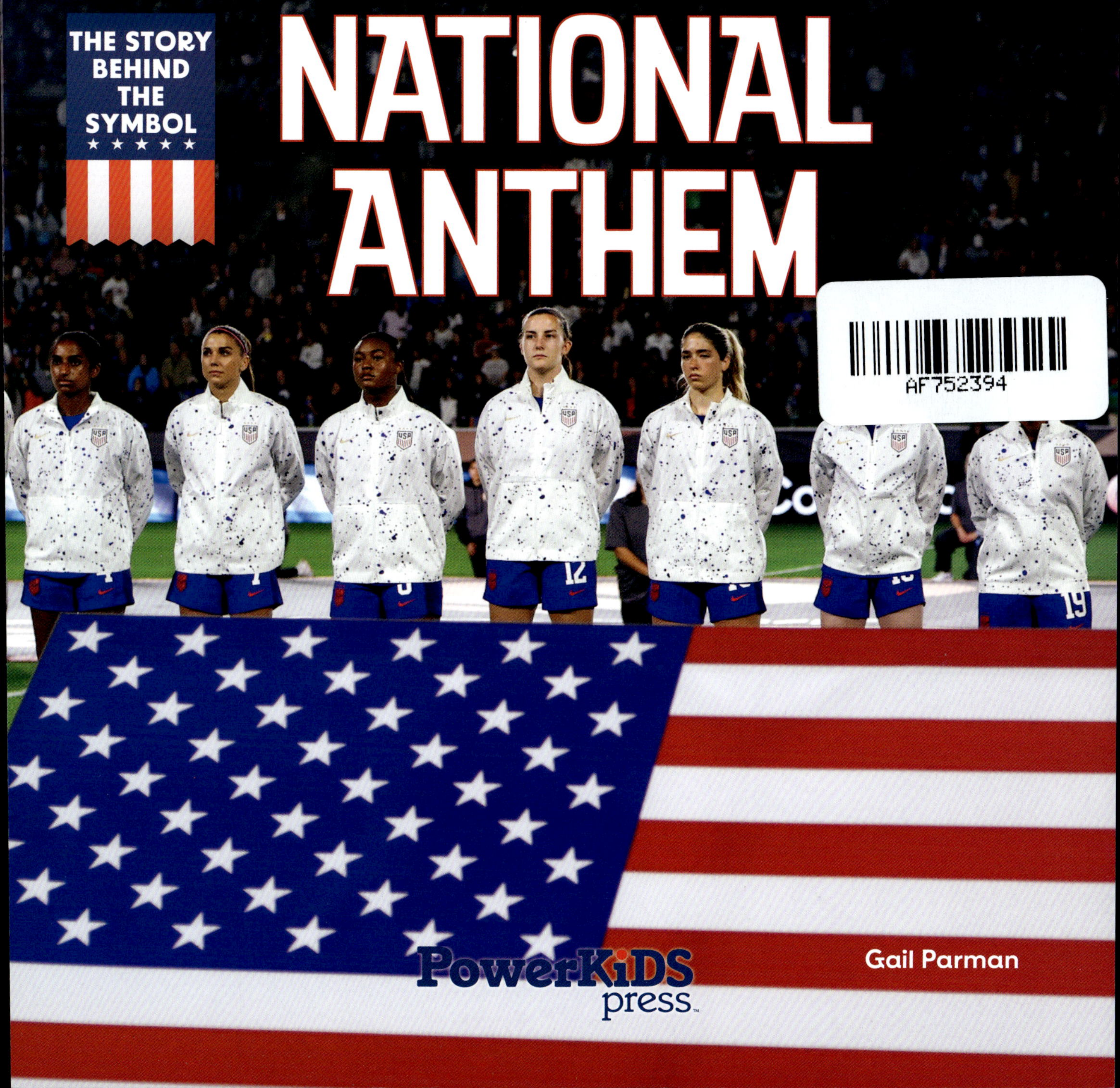

PowerKiDS press

Gail Parman

Published in 2027 by The Rosen Publishing Group, Inc.
2544 Clinton Street, Buffalo, NY 14224

Portions of this work were originally authored by Cecelia H. Brannon and published as *Zoom in on American Symbols: Zoom in on the National Anthem*. All new material in this edition is authored by Gail Parman.

Editor: Tricia Hoffman
Book Design: Beeline Media and Design

Photo Credits: Cover, p. 1 Ringo Chiu/Shutterstock.com; cover, p. 1, 5, 6, 9, 11, 13, 15, 17, 19, 21 Realstockvector/Shutterstock.com; p. 4, 17 Wikipedia/Wikipedia; p. 5, 8, 10, 12, 13, 14, 16 Library of Congress/Library of Congress; p. 6, 7 Everett Collection/Shutterstock.com; p. 9 Shutterstock AI Generator/Shutterstock.com; p. 11 Mark Heighes/Shutterstock.com; p. 15 Burtmaks/Shutterstock.com; p. 18 Conor P. Fitzgerald/Shutterstock.com; p. 19 Leonard Zhukovsky/Shutterstock.com; p. 21 Jon Bilous/Shutterstock.com

Cataloging-in-Publication Data
Names: Parman, Gail.
Title: National anthem / Gail Parman.
Description: Buffalo, New York : PowerKids Press, 2027. | Series: The story behind the symbol |
Includes glossary and index.
Identifiers: ISBN 9781499458107 (pbk.) | ISBN 9781499458114 (library bound) | ISBN 9781499458121 (ebook)
Subjects: LCSH: Key, Francis Scott, 1779-1843--Juvenile literature. | Star-spangled banner (Song)--Juvenile literature. |
National songs--United States--History and criticism--Juvenile literature.
Classification: LCC E356.B2 P377 2027 | DDC 782.4215990973--dc23

Printed in China

CPSIA Compliance Information: Batch #QSPK27. For Further Information contact Rosen Publishing at 1-800-237-9932.

CONTENTS

O Say Can You See

"The Star-Spangled Banner" is the national **anthem** of the United States. You probably know some of the words, but do you know its history?

Just 33 years after America separated from Britain and became a new nation, the United States went to war with Britain again. In September 1814, British troops began firing on Fort McHenry in the **harbor** of Baltimore. The bombing lasted 25 hours. Ships were destroyed. Nearly 1,800 bombs were fired at the fort. But as the shots stopped firing, the smoke cleared, the sun rose, and a large American flag was raised above the fort. The sight of the stars and stripes **inspired** one of the most famous poems in American history.

The War of 1812 began over fights about land. It became heated very fast.

The Bombs Bursting in Air

When the battle at Fort McHenry began, lawyer Francis Scott Key was on a British ship, working for the release of an American. For safety, he stayed on the ship several miles out into the harbor. He could only watch in horror as the fort was hit by rockets and bombs. But as dawn broke, and he saw the flag waving above the fort, he knew that the Americans had won the battle. He was so inspired that he began writing the poem right away. His words would later become the country's national **anthem**.

Francis Scott Key was a distant cousin of the famous writer F. Scott Fitzgerald, who was named after him.

F. Scott Fitzgerald

Francis Scott Key

FRANCIS SCOTT KEY

Francis Scott Key (known as "Frank" to family and friends) was born on August 1, 1779, in Maryland. His grandparents had come to America from England in 1726. His father served as a captain during the Revolutionary War. Frank attended St. John's College in Annapolis, Maryland, and became a lawyer in Baltimore. He and his wife, Mary Tayloe Lloyd, had 11 children.

Key enjoyed writing poetry. Most of his poems were religious, but his most famous poem is patriotic. He began writing it on the back of a letter while still on the ship in Baltimore Harbor. When finished, it was four **verses** long.

Only the first verse is used as the national anthem, but the entire poem is often read during public **ceremonies.**

The Poem Becomes a Song

Francis Scott Key's poem was originally titled "The Defence of Fort M'Henry." It became "The Star-Spangled Banner" a few months later when stores started selling it as sheet music.

The poem written by Francis Scott Key did not have a **melody** at first. It was simply a poem. But when Key gave a copy of his poem to Judge Joseph H. Nicholson, the judge noticed that the words fit perfectly with a popular English song, "The Anacreontic Song" by composer John Stafford Smith. It was then that Key's poem was set to music.

The melody of the song sounds different today than it did at first. The song was originally meant for a group of people to sing together, but many singers today perform it on their own.

Growing in Popularity

Years later, the song was a comfort to many Americans during the U.S. Civil War. It became more and more popular over the years.

By the 1890s, the military used the song whenever it raised or lowered the flag. It was played during the first game of the 1918 World Series, which began the tradition of the song being played before every game.

But the song did not officially become the anthem of the United States until 1931. Today, it is commonly heard at public events, such as parades and sporting events, across the country.

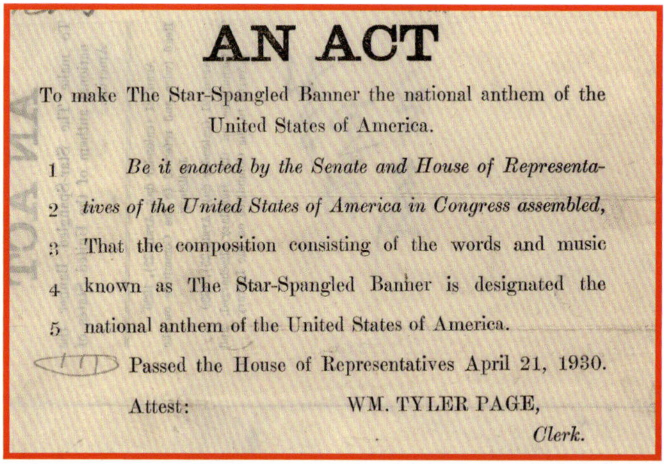

AN ACT

To make The Star-Spangled Banner the national anthem of the United States of America.

1 *Be it enacted by the Senate and House of Representa-*
2 *tives of the United States of America in Congress assembled,*
3 That the composition consisting of the words and music
4 known as The Star-Spangled Banner is designated the
5 national anthem of the United States of America.

Passed the House of Representatives April 21, 1930.

Attest: WM. TYLER PAGE,
Clerk.

President Herbert Hoover declared "The Star-Spangled Banner" the official national anthem of the United States in 1931.

Our Flag Was Still There

The flag that flew above Fort McHenry is called the Star-Spangled Banner because it inspired the **lyrics** to the famous song. It is a large **garrison** flag, meaning that it is bigger than most flags. It was meant to fly high and be seen from great distances.

The flag at Fort McHenry was sewn by hand by a widow named Mary Pickersgill. George Armistad, the commander of the fort, asked Pickersgill to sew the flag in 1813. It took her seven weeks. She had the help of her teenage daughters, Eliza and Mary Young, and a servant, Grace Wisher, who was 13.

Mary Pickersgill

Built in 1798, Fort McHenry is a star-shaped fort in Baltimore Harbor. It is named after James McHenry, a signer of the United States Constitution and secretary of war under Presidents Washington and Adams.

A National Treasure

The original flag is not the same as the flag we use today. Because the nation was still new in 1814, there were 15 stars and 15 stripes. Each star is about 24 inches (60 cm) across. Each of the red and white stripes is about 24 inches (60 cm) thick.

The flag is now a national treasure. It has been on display at the Smithsonian Museum of American History in Washington, D.C., since 1907. The museum will be the flag's permanent home. It is kept in a special case under temperature control and low lighting to help preserve the fragile fabric.

The original Star-Spangled Banner was 30 feet (9 m) tall and 42 feet (12 m) wide.

Respect the Anthem

The U.S. Flag Code states that whenever the anthem is played and the flag is displayed, every person present, except those in uniform, must stand at attention. They must face the flag with the right hand over the heart. Members of the military must salute, and hats should be removed as a sign of respect.

The song has been translated into many languages, including German, Hebrew, Spanish, Yiddish, French, Samoan, and Navajo. It reflects the **diversity** of people who make the United States what it is today.

Many famous American singers have performed "The Star-Spangled Banner." Jon Batiste, Demi Lovato, and Chris Stapleton have all been given the honor.

A Lasting Legacy

Today, "The Star-Spangled Banner" is often performed before sports events, military ceremonies, college graduations, and more. It is a powerful symbol of American unity and pride. The next time you hear it, you can think about its history, and how it came to be the song that represents the United States of America.

The Star-Spangled Banner

O say can you see, by the
dawn's early light,
What so proudly we hailed at
the twilight's last gleaming,
Whose broad stripes and
bright stars through the
perilous fight,
O'er the ramparts we
watched,
were so gallantly streaming?
And the rockets' red glare, the
bombs bursting in air,
Gave proof through the night
that our flag was still there;
O say does that star-span-
gled
banner yet wave
O'er the land of the free and
the home of the brave?

The Fracis Scott Key Bridge, which was destroyed in 2024, was built on the spot from where the British fired on Fort McHenry.

Activity: Write Your Anthem

A national anthem is a patriotic song that shows the history and traditions of a country and its people. But people can have anthems too! It can be any song of celebration that represents you. What would your anthem be? Grab some paper and try writing your own anthem!

1. First, think about the things or people that are most important to you. Who or what makes you *you*? Maybe it's music or soccer. Maybe it's your pet or your grandmother. Choose one of these to write about.

2. Write down all the words that come to mind when you think of this person or thing. Include words that show how you feel. Describe images that come to your mind.

3. Once you have a list of about 10 to 20 words and descriptions, try to put them together. Before you know it, you'll have your very own anthem. You can even try setting it to music and dancing along!

Glossary

anthem A patriotic song used by a country.

ceremony A formal gathering to celebrate an occasion.

diversity Including people of different races, cultures, and backgrounds.

garrison A group of soldiers who live in a fort to protect it.

harbor A place on the coast where many ships dock.

inspire To encourage someone to make or do something.

lyrics The words to a song.

melody The notes of a song.

verse A part of a poem or song.

Index

Learn More

Francis Scott Key
www.biography.com/authors-writers/francis-scott-key
Read more about the life and career of the writer of "The Star-Spangled Banner."

Visit the Star-Spangled Banner
https://amhistory.si.edu/starspangledbanner/visit.aspx
Find out how you can visit the Star-Spangled Banner Exhibition at the Smithsonian National Museum of American History.